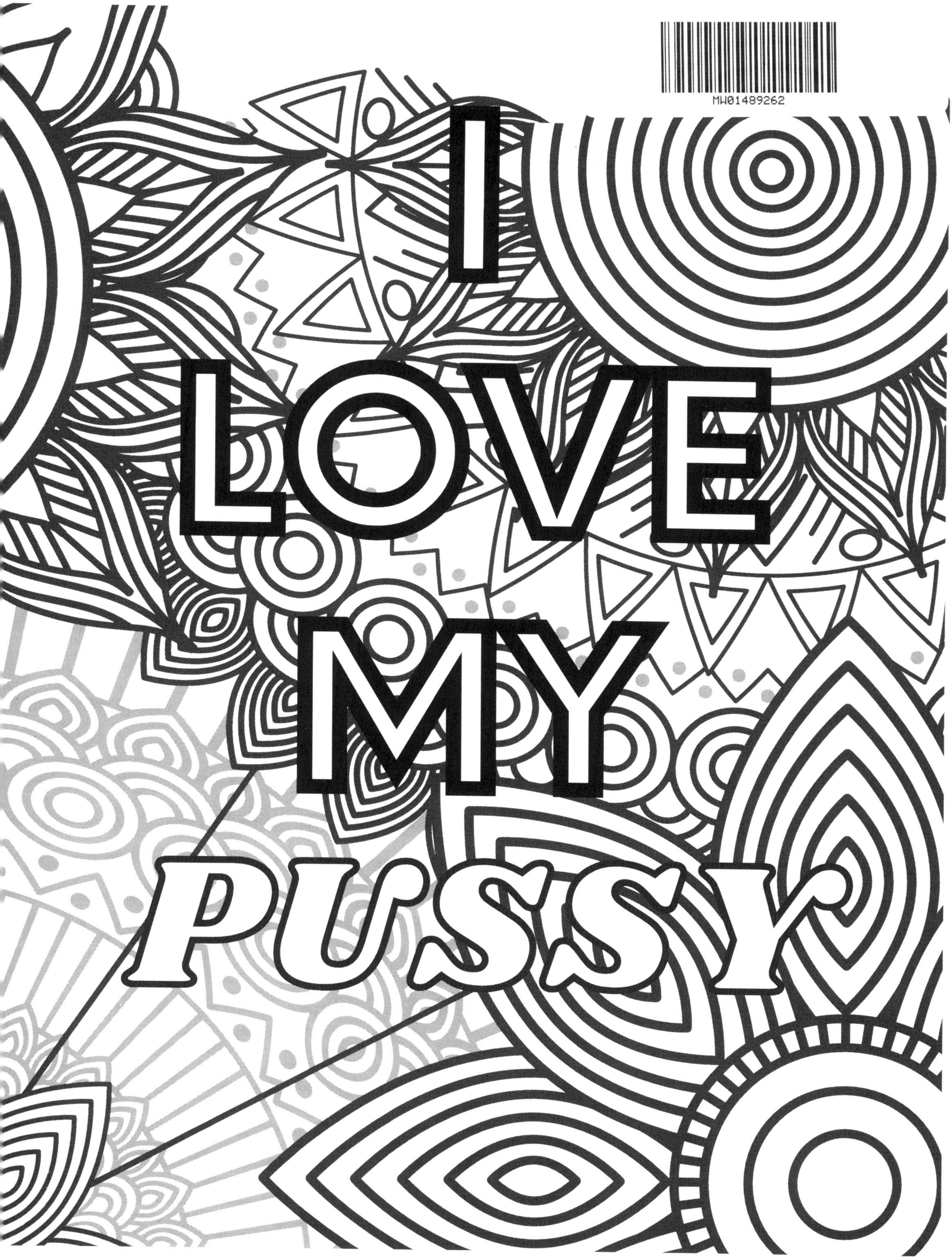
I
LOVE
MY
PUSSY

MY
PUSSY
MY
RULES!

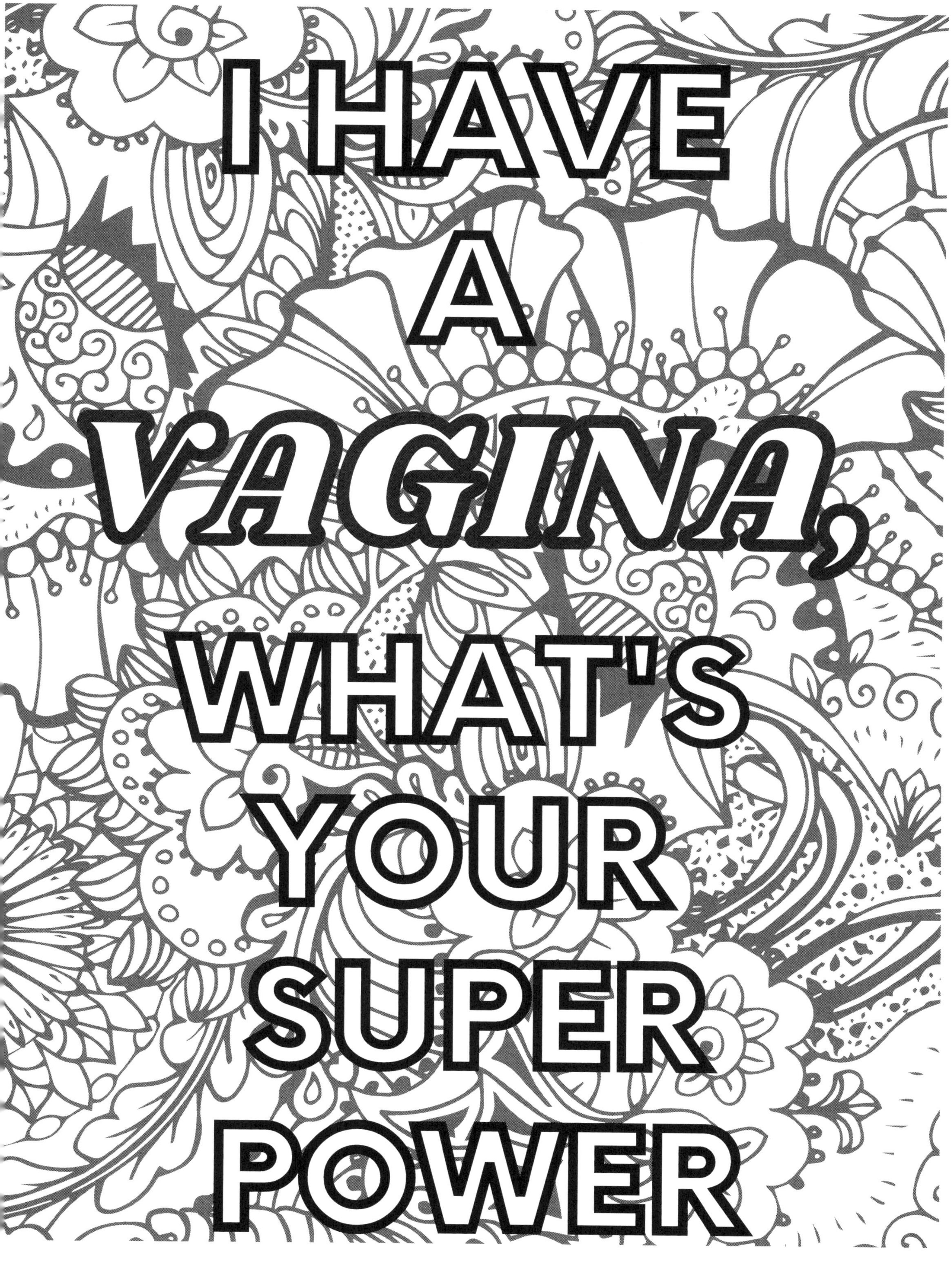
I HAVE
A
VAGINA,
WHAT'S
YOUR
SUPER
POWER

POWER
TO
THE
PUSSY

VAGINA'S,
THE
REASON
LIFE
EXIST

MY
PUSSY
IS
PERFECT

VAGINA
JOKES
AREN'T
FUNNY.
PERIOD.

BEST
PUSSY
EVER

I
HAVE A
VAGINA
HEAR ME
ROAR

PUSSY,
MORE
MAGICAL
THAN A
UNICORN

I
VALUE
MY
VAGINA

PUSSY
RUNS
THE
WORLD

MY VAGINA
IS
MY
BEST
FRIEND

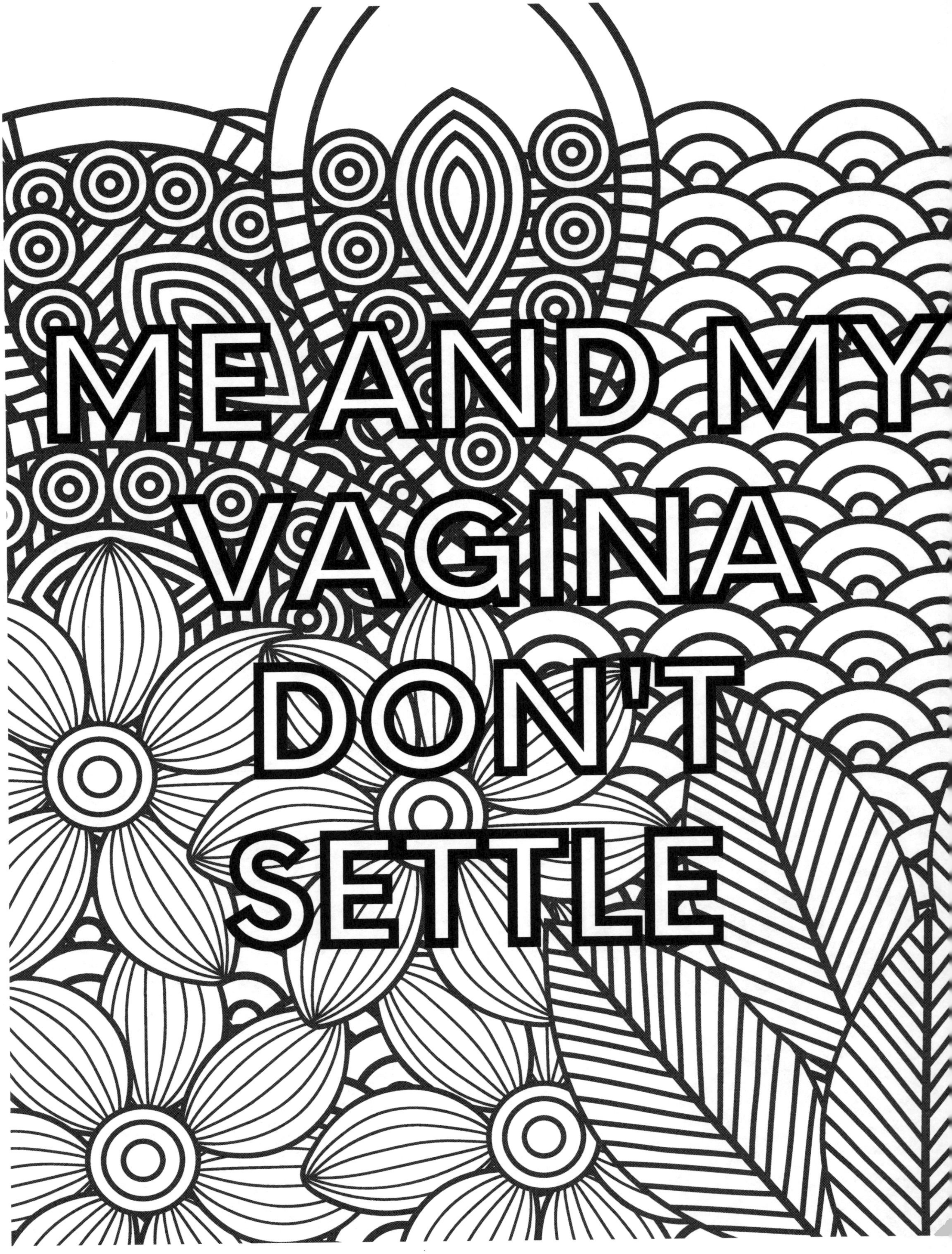
ME AND MY
VAGINA
DON'T
SETTLE

MY
VAGINA
IS
PERFECT

PROUD
OF
MY
PUSSY

I WILL
NEVER
APOLOGIZE
FOR HAVING A
VAGINA

PUSSY
PUSSY
PUSSY

VAGINA
VAGINA
VAGINA

MY
VAGINA
IS
BEAUTIFUL

MY
VAGINA
IS
PERFECT

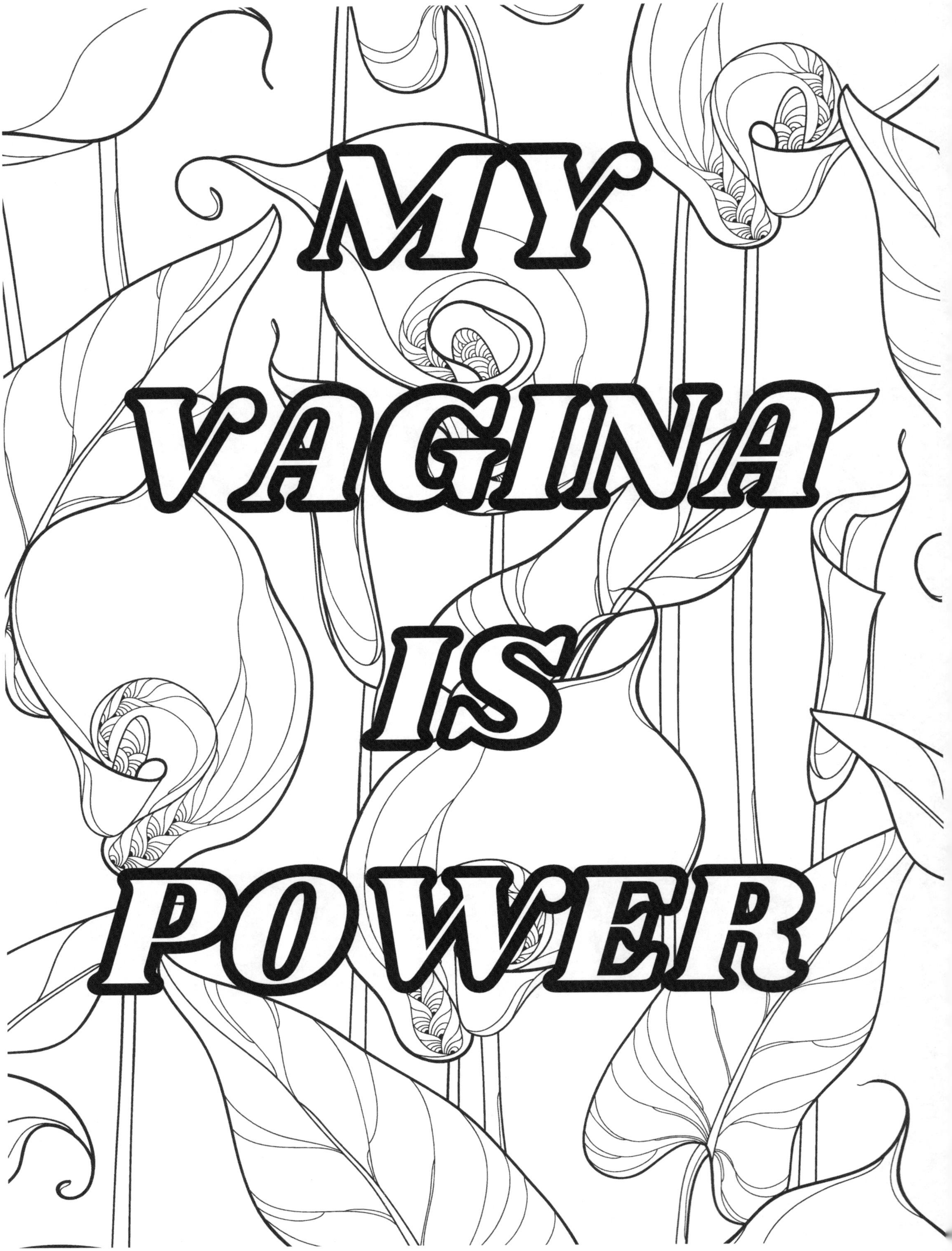
MY
VAGINA
IS
POWER

PUSSY
RUNS
THE
WORLD

VAGINA
AND
PUSSY

Made in the USA
Monee, IL
19 March 2025

14264829R00015